The Jolly Rascal

Published in the United States by
QEB Publishing, Inc.
23062 La Cadena Drive
Laguna Hills
Irvine
CA 92653

Library of Congress Control
Number 2004101904

ISBN 1-59566-013-5

Written by Clare Bevan
Designed by Alix Wood
Editor Hannah Ray
Illustrated by Angela Jolliffe

Series Consultant Anne Faundez
Creative Director Louise Morley
Editorial Manager Jean Coppendale

Printed and bound in China

START
Reading

The Jolly Rascal

Clare Bevan

QEB Publishing, Inc.

The Jolly Rascal sails away
Across the stormy sea,
With Captain Flo
And Big Bad Joe,
And Pirates One, Two, Three.

"Land ho! Land ho!" says Captain Flo.
"Let's look for gold," says Joe.
They flap, flap, flap
The treasure map,
The Pirates say, "Let's go!"

They crawl around the rocky ground,
They crawl around the trees
Where monsters peep,
Where tigers creep,
And Pirates rub their knees.

7

"Away we go," says Captain Flo.
"Away we go," says Joe,
"With me and you,
With Tiger, too,
And Pirates in a row."

They find a place where rivers race,
Where fishes swim about,
Where waters CRASH,
And ducks go SPLASH!
The Pirates say, "Look out!"

They find a bay where people say,
"We're glad you came this way...
Here's food for you
And Tiger, too."
The Pirates shout, "Hooray!"

"Follow me," says Captain Flo.
"Follow me," says Joe,
"Past hut and hole
And totem pole."
The Pirates shout, "Bravo!"

They stamp their feet to a jungle beat,
They find a magic fountain.
The Tiger passes
Stripy grasses
And Pirates climb a mountain.

13

"Up we go!" says Captain Flo.
"Up we go!" says Joe,
"Climb so high
We touch the sky."
The Pirates peer below.

They all look for a sandy shore,
They all look at the map...
Across the land
They spot the sand!
The Pirates cheer and clap.

Says Flo to Joe, "Sing yo, ho, ho!
The Jolly Rascal Song.
Dig far, dig low,
Dig fast, dig slow!"
The Pirates sing along.

They dig the sand with shovels and hands,
At last the treasure's here...
The golden rings,
The shiny things!
The Pirates clap and cheer.

17

"Home we go," says Captain Flo.
"Home we go," says Joe,
"With bags of gold
For us to hold."
The Pirates sing, "Yo, ho!"

The Jolly Rascal sails away
From sand and land and tree,
With Captain Flo
And Big Bad Joe,
And Pirates One, Two, Three.

So Captain Flo and Big Bad Joe,
They cross the sea so deep.
In time for tea,
Then happily...
The Pirates fall asleep.

What do you think?

Can you remember how many Pirates went to sea with Captain Flo and Big Bad Joe?

Captain Flo and Big Bad Joe meet some people in a bay. Who do you think these people are?

Where did Captain Flo, Big Bad Joe, and the Pirates find the buried treasure?

What happened when the Pirates arrived back home?

23

Parents' and teachers' notes

- Read the story to your child and talk about the adventure that Captain Flo, Big Bad Joe, and the Pirates have in the Jolly Rascal.
- Look at the pictures together. Do they tell a different story? Ask your child to describe what is happening in each picture.
- Hunt through the story for pirate-related words, for example, "treasure map," "Land ho!"
- How many words in the story begin with "p" for "pirate"? Count them with your child.
- Search for rhyming words. Have fun inventing more.
- Read The Jolly Rascal Song on page 16. Create a tune for the song and sing it together.
- Find a cardboard box and invent an adventure. For example, a ride in a spaceship, a submarine, a racing car, or a train.
- Together, write your own story. Encourage your child to draw and color pictures to accompany his/her text. Take it in turns to read the finished story out loud.
- What, in reality, is the pirates' jungle? (The back yard.) The stormy sea? (A rug on the floor.) The mountain? (The climbing frame and slide.) Where is the place where rivers race? (The bathroom.)
- Boost your child's confidence by looking for words that are easy to read; for example, "we," "go," "me."
- Look for words that are difficult to read, e.g. "mountain". Can you help each other find tricks that make the words easier to remember? For example, "m" looks like a little range of mountains.
- Read the story again together, and look out for that tiger!